Butterfly

Written by Jenny Feely
Photography by Michael Curtain

sundance

There was
a butterfly
on a leaf.

3

Then there was
an egg
on a leaf.

Then there was
a caterpillar
on a stem.

7

Then there was
a chrysalis
on a leaf.

Then there was
a new butterfly
on a leaf.

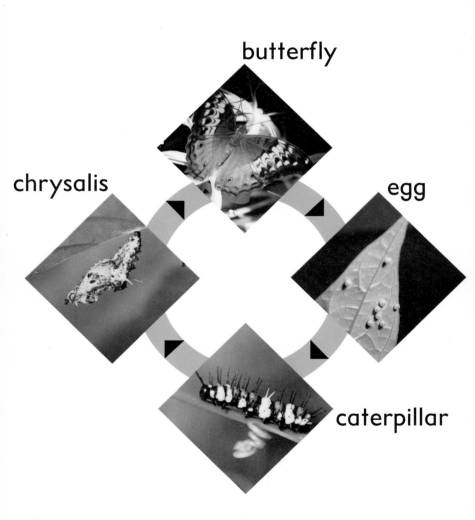

butterfly

chrysalis

egg

caterpillar